FOLLOWING JESUS IN THE MODERN WORLD BIBLE STUDY

GREG LAURIE

FOLLOWING JESUS IN THE MODERN WORLD

BIBLE STUDY

GREG LAURIE

NAVPRESS
Discipleship Inside Out®

KERYGMA
PUBLISHING

ALLEN
DAVID
BOOKS

Discipleship Inside Out®

NavPress is the publishing ministry of The Navigators, an international Christian organization and leader in personal spiritual development. NavPress is committed to helping people grow spiritually and enjoy lives of meaning and hope through personal and group resources that are biblically rooted, culturally relevant, and highly practical.

**For a free catalog go to www.NavPress.com
or call 1.800.366.7788 in the United States or 1.800.839.4769 in Canada.**

CONTENTS

GETTING STARTED

FOLLOWING JESUS HAS always been impossible — without God's help. However, life in the twenty-first century makes it uniquely hard. Following Jesus takes time in a world that values productivity in other areas. It takes focus in a world that bombards us with demands for attention. It takes priority in a world that offers so many other enticing options. Lots of people won't hesitate to tell you how stupid it is to follow Jesus — it's so last millennium, so linked to social views and historical events that you should be ashamed of.

The apostle Matthew knew how hard it was to follow Jesus in the first century. He himself faced big challenges, and he wrote his gospel for readers who faced big challenges too. This study guide offers you a chance to grow as a follower of Jesus by learning from Matthew and putting into practice what you learn. What exactly does it mean to follow Jesus? How do you get the power from God to do it, no matter what life throws at you? Those are the kinds of questions you'll explore.

This study is based on the book *Following Jesus in the Modern World*, by Greg Laurie. At the beginning of each study session, you'll see the chapters of *Following Jesus in the Modern*

Notes and Observations

World that you should read before your group meets. However, this study is designed to work even if you don't have time to read the book. As long as you have a Bible, you'll be fine. (You will, however, get more out of it if you read *Following Jesus in the Modern World* as you go along.)

USING THIS STUDY ON YOUR OWN

Ideally, you'll read the relevant chapters of *Following Jesus in the Modern World* before you dig in to the questions for each session. Don't feel you must hurry to put down answers for all of the questions. If God is talking to you through one question, stay there and pray about it or write all that comes to you. This isn't a task to complete; it's a chance for you and God to talk about your life. If you skip some questions but you've been with God, that's what matters.

USING THIS STUDY WITH A GROUP

Again, ideally, you'll read the relevant chapters of *Following Jesus in the Modern World* before each meeting. Even better, read the chapters and spend some time thinking about answers to the questions before you meet. Better still, write your answers before the group meets. Then when you meet, don't just share what you've written—discuss it. Questions and different views are okay. You can certainly have a productive discussion without prior preparation, but you'll get much more out of the study if you make time for at least the reading at home.

Do establish a discussion leader. This person's job is to keep the conversation moving and decide when to go to the next question. He or she doesn't need to have the answers. If you are chosen for this role, see the Leader's Notes at the end of this guide. There are tips for guiding a discussion as well as ideas for individual questions.

Sometimes you may find it helpful to have someone read aloud the text between the questions. That text includes excerpts

from *Following Jesus in the Modern World* that help to frame the
questions. Reading aloud is especially helpful if people haven't
had time to read the material on their own and write answers to
the questions.

Do read aloud the Bible passages, whether you are looking
them up in your Bible or they are printed in this book.

Finally, be as honest as you can with the members of your
group. If you want to grow spiritually, you will greatly benefit
from having other people who know what's going on with you
and are supporting you, praying for you, and challenging your
thinking.

Notes and Observations

1
WHAT DOES FOLLOWING MEAN?

To prepare for this discussion, please read chapters 1 and 2 of *Following Jesus in the Modern World*.

IF YOU SAY you are a follower of Jesus, what does that mean? Does it mean that you check your phone a lot to see if He's posted any news about His ideas or His personal life? Or that you stay up to date on the celebrity gossip about Him? Or that you spend an hour a week singing songs about Him? Does it mean that you like Him, or agree with Him on politics, or are counting on Him to guarantee you a comfy life after death no matter how you run your life before death?

Over and over in the Bible, when Jesus wanted someone to join His team, He said, "Follow Me." If He said it so much, it makes sense for us to find out what He meant. That's what we'll do in this session.

Notes and Observations

Notes and Observations

1. When you were a child, who was someone you followed? Maybe you followed your mom around when you were very small. Or you tried to copy an older sibling. Or maybe there was a leader at school. Or maybe you were the leader and others followed your lead. Was there a superhero you wanted to follow? Or were you a loner who followed no one?

In chapters 5 through 7 of Matthew's gospel, Jesus gave a series of instructions to His followers. He ended with these words:

> *Not everyone who says to Me, "Lord, Lord," shall enter the kingdom of heaven, but he who does the will of My Father in heaven. Many will say to Me in that day, "Lord, Lord, have we not prophesied in Your name, cast out demons in Your name, and done many wonders in Your name?" And then I will declare to them, "I never knew you; depart from Me, you who practice lawlessness!" (Matthew 7:21-23)*

> *Anyone who listens to my teaching and follows it is wise, like a person who builds a house on solid rock. Though the rain comes in torrents and the floodwaters rise and the winds beat against that house, it won't collapse because it is built on bedrock. (Matthew 7:24-25, NLT)*

2. What can we learn from Matthew 7:21-25 about what it does and doesn't mean to follow Jesus?

Does mean:

Doesn't mean:

3. What are some examples of doing the will of Jesus' Father? (You can look at Matthew 5:21–6:34 for ideas.)

The phrase *follow Me* is a fascinating expression in the Greek. It comes from the word that means "to walk the same road." To follow Jesus, then, means you walk the same road as He walks. And because that word is in the imperative mode, it is not just an invitation; it is a command. In addition, the verb is in the present tense, commanding the beginning of an action and continuing habitually in it.

So what does that add up to when we put it all together?

Jesus was saying, "I command you to follow Me each and every day." (*Following Jesus in the Modern World*, 16)

Jesus wants to be a part of everything that you do. He's not just a Sunday Jesus, but an everyday Jesus. He wants to go with you to church and to school and to work. He wants to be at your side when you're at the movies or on the Internet. Jesus wants to go with you wherever you go. (*Following Jesus in the Modern World*, 17)

4. What might it look like for you to follow Jesus when you are . . .

at work or school?

on the Internet?

dealing with your family?

5. Read Matthew 9:9-13. To follow Jesus, Matthew had to walk away from a highly paid but corrupt career collecting taxes for Rome. What are some things a person today might have to walk away from in order to follow Jesus? (In addition to big things like certain careers, think of habits, too.)

A follower of Jesus can't say good-bye to the old life fast enough. . . . And let me add this: Whatever you give up to follow Jesus will be replaced by something far better. Sometimes I will hear people say, "I gave up a friendship to follow Jesus." Or, "I broke off a relationship with my boyfriend," or, "I gave up my career."

Yes, and God will make it up to you, in this life and in the life to come . . . but especially in the life to come. (*Following Jesus in the Modern World*, 27)

6. Have you ever had to walk away from something in order to follow Jesus? If so, what has God given you that is far better?

A follower of Jesus cares about unbelievers and wants to reach them.

Again, I love the example of Matthew. Using his influence and his wealth and his network of friends, he threw a huge party and brought in Jesus Christ as the guest speaker! Reaching his friends and colleagues was the first thing he wanted to do after he became a follower of Jesus. (*Following Jesus in the Modern World*, 27–28)

7. What challenges do followers of Jesus today have to overcome in order to reach unbelievers?

A follower of Jesus loves Him more than anyone or anything else.

Jesus is number one in this person's life, even if it means the painful severing of other relationships. What's more, a true follower of Jesus is always on guard against those temptations, habits, attitudes, activities, or associations that would grieve the Lord or steal away their love for Him. (*Following Jesus in the Modern World*, 28)

Notes and Observations

8. "Severing other relationships" doesn't mean avoiding relationships with all unbelievers. If it did, we couldn't reach unbelievers. So what sorts of relationships might a person need to end in order to put Jesus first?

When Jesus' disciples followed Him, at one point that path led directly into a storm.

Now when He got into a boat, His disciples followed Him. And suddenly a great tempest arose on the sea, so that the boat was covered with the waves. But He was asleep. Then His disciples came to Him and awoke Him, saying, "Lord, save us! We are perishing!"

But He said to them, "Why are you fearful, O you of little faith?" Then He arose and rebuked the winds and the sea, and there was a great calm. So the men marveled, saying, "Who can this be, that even the winds and the sea obey Him?" (Matthew 8:23-27)

9. How did the disciples respond when the storm hit? What were their emotions? Their actions?

Storms are normal when we follow Jesus. God has purposes in these storms: (1) to correct us when we've done something wrong, or (2) to protect us from something worse, or most often (3) to perfect us to be more like Jesus. We may never know the purpose of a particular storm this side of heaven, but it has a purpose. And whether or not Jesus stops the storm, He is always with us in it. Our job is to cry out to Him in the midst of our storms.

10. What are the various ways we can respond when a storm (a tragedy, an illness or injury, a job loss, etc.) hits our lives? List the range of emotions we may have and things we may do, both negative and positive.

11. What if we can't feel Jesus' presence with us in the midst of a storm? Are we doing something wrong? Is He doing something wrong? How should we deal with not feeling His presence?

"[The disciples] cried out, 'Lord save us!'" [Matthew 8:25]. And by the way, I don't think they whispered those words.

When I say cry out to Jesus, I mean *cry out* — whatever is on your heart. You will never offend God by raising your voice. Tell Him just how you're feeling. He already knows!

God, why?

God, what?

God, where are You?

Lord, I don't get this.

Lord, I don't like this.

Lord, this is really hard.

Jesus, this doesn't make any sense to me.

Lord, HELP!

All of those expressions are perfectly legitimate. In fact, you can read prayers of much greater intensity in the book of Psalms.

Sometimes I think we feel as though we need to sanitize our prayers or pretty them up a little. No, God wants to hear you speak from your heart. He wants honest

Notes and Observations

prayer, even if it's shouted or cried out through tears. Again, read the honesty of David and others in the Psalms as they cried out to God, pouring out their frustration to Him. Even Jesus, hanging on the cross, said, "My God, My God, why have You forsaken Me?" . . .

[Sometimes] God will let us get to the very end of our rope, coming to the end of ourselves, so that we might (finally) cry out to Him. (*Following Jesus in the Modern World*, 33–34)

12. Why is it essential to cry out to Jesus in the midst of a storm?

13. How do you respond to the idea of shouting or weeping in prayer to God? Why?

14. What is the most important thing you'd like to pray for right now? Do you want to . . .

- Ask for Jesus' help in following Him in your work or some other area of your life?
- Ask for His strength and courage to walk away from a harmful relationship or habit?
- Ask Him to reveal Himself to an unbeliever you know?
- Cry out to Him in the midst of a storm?
- Ask for something else?

If you're doing this study on your own, write out your prayer, or speak it aloud. Don't be embarrassed to be honest. If you're meeting with a group, briefly explain how they can pray for you. Then take time to pray for one another.

Notes and Observations

2
DOUBT AND TRUST

To prepare for this discussion, please read chapters
3 through 5 of *Following Jesus in the Modern World*.

SOME PEOPLE IMAGINE that following Jesus means having
all of the right beliefs about Him and never struggling with
questions. This is misguided on two counts. On the one hand,
as we'll see in Matthew's gospel, the demons actually had a lot
of right beliefs about Jesus. They knew doctrine better than a
lot of Christians. (And that's sad.)

On the other hand, we'll also see that in times of stress and
growth even faithful servants of God have doubts and questions.
Doubts can be a sign that we're thinking, while lack of questions can indicate that we're disengaged from the living God
and we're just going through the motions.

So let's look at the difference between saving faith and mere
assent to right beliefs. And then let's look at how lively faith can
flourish even in times of doubt.

Notes and Observations

1. If you could ask Jesus one question right now and get an answer, what would you ask?

Here is Matthew's account of what happened right after Jesus calmed the storm on the Sea of Galilee:

> When He had come to the other side, to the country of the Gergesenes, there met Him two demon-possessed men, coming out of the tombs, exceedingly fierce, so that no one could pass that way. And suddenly they cried out, saying, "What have we to do with You, Jesus, You Son of God? Have You come here to torment us before the time?"
>
> Now a good way off from them there was a herd of many swine feeding. So the demons begged Him, saying, "If You cast us out, permit us to go away into the herd of swine."
>
> And He said to them, "Go." So when they had come out, they went into the herd of swine. And suddenly the whole herd of swine ran violently down the steep place into the sea, and perished in the water.
>
> Then those who kept them fled; and they went away into the city and told everything, including what had happened to the demon-possessed men. And behold, the whole city came out to meet Jesus. And when they saw Him, they begged Him to depart from their region.
>
> So He got into a boat, crossed over, and came to His own city. (Matthew 8:28–9:1)

2. What do you think the demons meant when they called Jesus "Son of God" in Matthew 8:29?

3. They also asked, "Have You come here to torment us before the time?" What did they mean by "the time"? What Bible teachings did they apparently know and agree with?

If I were able to interview the devil (and I'm not applying for that job), I think we might be surprised at some of the things he would say.

I would ask him, "Do you believe in the existence of God?"

And he would say, "Yes, I do."

"Do you believe in the deity of Jesus Christ?"

"Yes, I do."

"Do you believe that the Bible is the Word of God?"

"Yes. I hate every word of it, but I believe it."

"Do you believe that Jesus Christ is coming back again?"

"Yes, I do."

"Do you believe there is a final judgment for you and your demons that follow you?"

"Yes, I do."

Just because you believe something is true, however, doesn't mean you have submitted your life to that truth. Demons are in open rebellion against God, but they know truth. Satan and his fallen angels certainly believe. Evil spirits may number in the millions, but there isn't an atheist or an agnostic in the bunch. They *know*. The apostle James wrote, "You believe that there is one God. Good! Even the demons believe that — and shudder" (James 2:19, NIV).

Actually the word *shudder* could also be translated "to bristle." It conveys the picture of some horror that causes the hair to stand on end. (*Following Jesus in the Modern World*, 56–57)

4. How is *knowing* that Jesus is the Son of God different from *submitting your life* to the truth that Jesus is the Son of God? What does submitting your life to that truth involve?

Shortly thereafter, Matthew tells us these two interwoven stories of people who needed Jesus' help:

A ruler came and worshiped Him, saying, "My daughter has just died, but come and lay Your hand on her and she will live." So Jesus arose and followed him, and so did His disciples.

And suddenly, a woman who had a flow of blood for twelve years came from behind and touched the hem of His garment. For she said to herself, "If only I may touch His garment, I shall be made well." But Jesus turned around, and when He saw her He said, "Be of good cheer, daughter; your faith has made you well." And the woman was made well from that hour.

When Jesus came into the ruler's house, and saw the flute players and the noisy crowd wailing, He said to them, "Make room, for the girl is not dead, but sleeping." And they ridiculed Him. But when the crowd was put outside, He went in and took her by the hand, and the girl arose. And the report of this went out into all that land. (Matthew 9:18-26)

The synagogue ruler was an important man. The woman was an outcast because bleeding made her unclean for temple worship, and anyone who touched her was also unclean. Both were suffering and desperate.

5. How did the bleeding woman demonstrate the kind of faith Jesus wanted to see? How was her faith different from the "belief" that the demons had?

In Mark's longer version of the story, the synagogue ruler (whose name is Jairus) first approached Jesus when his daughter was still alive, and only later learned she had died.

> I have been in that place too, when I got news about my own son Christopher being killed in a traffic accident. There is just no way to explain what it feels like. It's as though your life has just ended — but even worse, because you wish it *had* ended.
>
> Because of my own experience, I have a sense of what Jairus was going through when he got this message: "Don't bother Jesus anymore, Jairus. It's over. She just died." . . .
>
> I think [the woman's interruption] was a test in the life of Jairus. How would he fare? . . . *I don't like this interruption, but I know this is the way Jesus is. He takes time with needy people. I'm not going to create any trouble here. I'll just wait on Him. He knows what He is doing.* (Following Jesus in the Modern World, 73–74)

6. What thoughts, feelings, and questions about God can arise when we get terrible news?

7. How did the synagogue ruler demonstrate faith in Jesus? The text in Matthew 9 doesn't tell us anything he did after verse 18, but what are some of the things he *didn't* do?

> If you trust in Jesus, your stories will have a happy ending.
>
> You might say, "What are you talking about, Greg? Are you living in the same world I'm living in?"
>
> Yes, as a matter of fact, I am.
>
> And I've had my share of suffering and sorrow in life. So how can I . . . tell you that your story will have a happy ending? It's because I believe in heaven.
>
> Your story will not be over at the end of your life on earth. In fact, if you belong to Jesus Christ, your story will be just beginning in eternity, in the presence of God. This is where every follower of Jesus will have a happy ending.
> (*Following Jesus in the Modern World*, 83)

8. How does the promise of a happy ending in heaven affect you right now? Does it cause you great joy? Courage? A shrug? Does it seem terribly far away compared to what is going on in your story today? Explain.

9. How do you think Jesus views people who are discouraged and are having trouble feeling great about a happy ending in heaven?

Matthew 11 tells us that John the Baptist dealt with that kind of discouragement. He was in prison for speaking truth to powerful people: King Herod and his sister-in-law/niece Herodias, whom Herod had illicitly "married." The prophet Isaiah had promised that the Messiah would proclaim freedom for the captives (see Isaiah 61:1), yet there was John, sitting in prison and likely to be executed any day. So John had a question:

And when John had heard in prison about the works of Christ, he sent two of his disciples and said to Him, "Are You the Coming One, or do we look for another?"

Jesus answered and said to them, "Go and tell John the things which you hear and see: The blind see and the lame walk; the lepers are cleansed and the deaf hear; the dead are raised up and the poor have the gospel preached to them. And blessed is he who is not offended because of Me." (Matthew 11:2-6)

10. In response to John's question, Jesus pointed to His own actions in words that echoed Isaiah 35:4-6 and 61:1. Read Isaiah 35:4-6. Why would that passage have been helpful to John?

In [Matthew 11:6, Jesus] used the occasion to make a point about persevering in faith: "Blessed is he who is not offended because of Me." Or literally, "Blessed is the man or woman who is not annoyed or repelled or made to stumble, whatever may occur." In essence, Jesus was saying, "Look, you may not understand My methods or My ways or My timing. But I am asking you to trust Me, even when you are unable to see why I am doing what I am doing — or why I'm *not* doing what you think I ought

Notes and Observations

to be doing. Just trust Me, hang in there, and hold your course." (*Following Jesus in the Modern World*, 95)

11. Why should we trust Jesus even when we don't understand why He's not doing what we expect?

12. Jesus went on to praise John (see Matthew 11:7-11). Why do you suppose Jesus wasn't hard on John for doubting Him?

Oswald Chambers once said, "Doubt is not always a sign that a man is wrong; it may be a sign that he is thinking."

Most of us, if we were honest, could admit to times when we doubted God and doubted our faith. Sometimes things happen in our lives that seem to make no earthly sense. In the midst of these experiences, we wonder where God is and why He permitted these things to happen in our lives. Or perhaps we come to a crucial crossroads where we desperately need an answer from God, but heaven seems silent and unresponsive to our cries.

We wonder, *Is God just sitting on His hands, watching me twist in the wind? Is He paying any attention to me at all?* And in such moments, we may (at least momentarily) entertain a few doubts. (*Following Jesus in the Modern World*, 85)

13. **How do you think we should respond when people share their doubts about God with us?**

Sometimes doubt is not the opposite of faith; it is rather an element of faith. It means you are thinking some things through and grappling with the issues. It means you are trying to process certain events or information, wondering how it all fits in with life as you understand it.

Sometimes you and I have to pass through the foyer of doubt to enter the sanctuary of certainty. That's something to keep in mind if your kids come to you and say, "Mom, I'm struggling with this. How can you say that God created the world?" Or, "Dad, I'm having a hard time with what the Bible says about living morally." Or, "My teacher says there are lots of contradictions in the Bible." Don't panic. That can be a good sign. It means they are starting to grow up and think for themselves, and you need to be available to help them through this process of finding their own faith. They can't live off the faith of their parents.

The key, however, in this matter of dealing with doubts is to cry out to God. . . .

Doubt, then, is a matter of the mind. Unbelief is a matter of the will. Doubt says, "I don't get it. Help me understand this. Work with me through this."

Unbelief says, "I do get it, I don't like it, and I refuse to accept it." (*Following Jesus in the Modern World*, 92–93)

Notes and Observations

14. How can we tell from Matthew 11:1-11 that John the Baptist had doubt, not unbelief?

> I think there are many times, possibly more times than we imagine, when we continue to wrestle with problems and situations simply because we have neglected to cry out to God for help.
>
> Have you prayed about your problem? Have you talked to the Lord about your medical condition? Your finances? Your marriage? Your seemingly mountain-sized problems? . . .
>
> Is there a decision you need wisdom on? Have you prayed for wisdom? . . .
>
> He may give you what you ask for; He may say, "Not now," or He may say, "No, My child, that wouldn't be good for you now. You have to trust Me to do the best for you." Then again, He may give you abundantly above and beyond what you ask for.
>
> The important thing is to call out to Him. (*Following Jesus in the Modern World*, 81–82)

15. What do you need to call out to Jesus about? Do you have a need like the bleeding woman or the synagogue ruler? Do you have a question like John the Baptist? If you're meeting with a group, share your need or question. Consider dividing into subgroups of three or four people to call out to God on each other's behalf. If it's the same thing you prayed about at your last meeting, that's fine. Persistence in prayer is a good thing.

If you're studying on your own, find someplace where you can't be overheard, and speak your need or question aloud. Don't edit yourself to sound holy. Just say it.

Notes and Observations

3

COME TO ME

To prepare for this discussion, please read chapters 6 and 7 of *Following Jesus in the Modern World*.

ONE OF THE ways we know we're following Jesus is when our lives are bearing good spiritual fruit. Spiritual fruit isn't something we can make simply by trying really, really hard. It's something that grows from us over time as we stay consistently rooted in Jesus. Spiritual fruit includes:

- What we say—praising God, verbally expressing love for others.
- Conduct and character (actions and inner life) that reflect joyful, peaceful, patient, self-controlled love.
- Winning others to Christ and helping them grow.

These things happen when we're habitually, all day long, rooted in Jesus. How do we go about that, especially when modern life is so unbelievably busy? That's what we'll consider in this session.

Come to Me, all you who labor and are heavy laden, and I will give you rest. Take My yoke upon you and learn from Me, for I am gentle and lowly in heart, and you will find rest

Notes and Observations

for your souls. For My yoke is easy and My burden is light.
(Matthew 11:28-30)

These words from Jesus are for every person in every place with any problem. . . . Nevertheless, this isn't an invitation to lazy people. He's speaking to people who labor and are heavy laden. To be weary implies that you've worked very hard — even to the point of exhaustion. I personally believe that Christians should be the hardest workers of all, no matter what the task. In 2 Thessalonians 3:12-13, the Bible tells believers to "settle down and work to earn their own living. . . . Never get tired of doing good" (NLT).

The Lord isn't speaking to unmotivated people here. He is speaking to weary people. He is addressing those who feel loaded down — and nearly crushed — by the weights and burdens of life. (*Following Jesus in the Modern World*, 107–108)

1. On a scale of 0 to 10, how loaded down with work and the burdens of life are you right now?

When I am burdened, when I am overwhelmed with worries, I need to come to Jesus with them. There is really nowhere else to go. . . .

Jesus simply said, "Come to Me."

He didn't say, "Study My teachings," though coming to Him includes that. He simply offered a wide-open invitation to approach Him, to be near to Him, and to have fellowship with Him. . . .

Our modern culture would say something very different. It would say, "Well, if you can just get that promotion . . .

if you can just buy that house . . . if you can just get married . . . if you can just take that two-week cruise . . . if you can just lease that expensive sports car . . . then you will find rest and be happy." (*Following Jesus in the Modern World*, 115–117)

2. Being near Jesus requires spending time with Him — talking to Him, listening to Him, reading Scripture, worshipping Him. How is that possible when our lives are so busy?

3. Do our lives have more time and space for Jesus if we don't look to material things, career advancement, or pleasure for rest and happiness? Or do the mere basics of keeping our families functional fill our days anyway? Explain your view.

The word Jesus uses here for *rest* is an interesting one. It is used elsewhere in the New Testament to describe chains falling off someone's hands. It carries with it the idea of being released from any kind of bondage. The child of God should not be under any kind of legalism, any kind of vice, or any kind of enslaving habit. . . .

Jesus [also] wants to release us from our debt of sin and all its life-destroying consequences and repercussions. If we have placed our faith in Christ, the Bible says we have been *justified*. Our sins have been forgiven, and the righteousness of Christ now has been placed into our account.

Finally, in Greek literature that same word used for *rest* is used to describe a door you can't quite open that

Notes and Observations

suddenly flies wide open. It's like gaining access to an area you never were able to enter before. . . . You and I have "backstage access" to God the Father through His Son, Jesus Christ. You can call upon Him at any time. If you wake up at three in the morning, the Lord is not asleep. He is ready to hear your cry and your prayer. (*Following Jesus in the Modern World*, 109–110)

4. How are these kinds of rest different from entertainment?

5. Which of these kinds of rest have you been especially grateful for in the past? Which do you most need today?

6. "Take My yoke upon you" (verse 29) means "Give Me the steering wheel of your life." What are some practical ways of doing that during a typical day?

Sometimes we . . . *say* that we have yielded the steering wheel of our lives to the Lord, but we still try to do a lot of backseat driving. *"Lord, speed up, speed up. Turn right. No, Lord, get us out of this lane—I don't like this lane. Oh . . . make a U-turn and go back, Lord. Let's not go this way."*

But He is saying, "Give Me the steering wheel." . . . It means submitting yourself to Christ every day in every way. . . .

But before you bristle at that idea, consider this. Everyone is yoked to something or someone. . . . It then becomes a question of who or what do you want to yoke your life to? Some are yoked to the power of sin and live under its power and control through all their days. I don't want to be under that power because I know it would shame me, wound my family and friends, shred my integrity, destroy my testimony for Jesus, and eventually kill me. Who wants to live like that? (*Following Jesus in the Modern World*, 111–112)

7. Think of a time when you had trouble giving Jesus the steering wheel of your life. What was it about that situation that made it so hard for you to submit to Jesus?

Now, when I think of a yoke around my neck and shoulders, I don't think of something that is light. The word *light,* however, could be better translated as "well fitting" or "easy to wear." The carpenter would custom-design each yoke for the particular ox that would be wearing it. In the same way, when you are committed to the Lord and submitted to His plan for your life, the yoke He gives to you just fits! It isn't burdensome at all. (*Following Jesus in the Modern World*, 113–114)

Notes and Observations

8. Do the things the Lord tells you to do make your life more burdensome or less? Give an example.

Jesus says, "Come to Me" (11:28) and "Learn from Me" (11:29). Then later He tells a parable about different ways people respond to what they hear from Him:

"Behold, a sower went out to sow. And as he sowed, some seed fell by the wayside; and the birds came and devoured them. Some fell on stony places, where they did not have much earth; and they immediately sprang up because they had no depth of earth. But when the sun was up they were scorched, and because they had no root they withered away. And some fell among thorns, and the thorns sprang up and choked them. But others fell on good ground and yielded a crop: some a hundredfold, some sixty, some thirty. He who has ears to hear, let him hear!" (Matthew 13:3-9)

What, then, is the determining factor in your spiritual growth as a believer in Christ?

You are.

It isn't up to God; it's up to you. . . .

Although He has provided us with mighty resources to enable us to grow and to help us grow, the ultimate decision on whether we *will* grow belongs to you and me.

The simple fact is, if you don't want to grow in the Lord or if you don't really care whether you grow in the Lord, you will find a million reasons why you can't do it. . . . We will make time for what is truly important to us. (*Following Jesus in the Modern World*, 120)

9. How do you respond to the idea that we make time for what is truly important to us? How true is that in your experience? Are there things you devote time to that are not important to you? Are there things that are truly important to you that you don't find time for (and if so, does that mean they're not really so important to you)?

In His parable, Jesus gave four categories of soil, or listeners. Category 1 is "Highway Hearers."

When anyone hears the word of the kingdom, and does not understand it, then the wicked one comes and snatches away what was sown in his heart. This is he who received seed by the wayside. (Matthew 13:19)

———————————————

The people I call "highway hearers" are those who might hear the Word, but they have allowed their hearts to become cold and hard. Where is the easiest place to get a hardened heart? The answer might surprise you. It's not in a bar, and it's not hanging around godless people who are doing godless things. In fact, the easiest place to get a hardened heart is in church.

As I have said many times before, the same sun that softens the wax hardens the clay. If you go to a church service or a Bible study with an attitude that says, "I don't want to hear this," your heart will be become just a little bit harder and less responsive. . . .

The lesson for all of us is to keep our hearts pliant and receptive by remaining open to hearing the Word of God and quickly responding to the voice of God's Holy Spirit. (*Following Jesus in the Modern World*, 126–127)

10. Why do you suppose someone would go to a Bible study if they don't want to do what the Bible passage says to do? What else might they want from Bible study or church?

The second type of soil is "Rocky Road Hearers."

But he who received the seed on stony places, this is he who hears the word and immediately receives it with joy; yet he has no root in himself, but endures only for a while. For when tribulation or persecution arises because of the word, immediately he stumbles. (Matthew 13:20-21)

There are those who seem to understand the Word and initially receive it with enthusiasm. But their response is a mile wide and an inch deep. The truth never really takes root. . . .

Becoming a Christian isn't about the emotion of the moment; it's about the test of time. . . . A person who thinks that every day with the Lord will be a big emotional rush will sooner or later wake up disappointed, because the emotions won't be there.

That's a critical moment in the Christian life, because God is saying to us that it's time to grow up and start walking by faith rather than by feelings. (*Following Jesus in the Modern World*, 127–129)

11. Have you ever had to walk by faith when you didn't feel God's presence for an extended period of time, or you felt afraid or embarrassed or angry because people were giving you a hard time about your commitment to Jesus? If so, what did walking by faith involve?

The third category of soil is "Thorny Hearers."

Now he who received seed among the thorns is he who hears the word, and the cares of this world and the deceitfulness of riches choke the word, and he becomes unfruitful. (Matthew 13:22)

_____

A "thorny hearer" is a person who receives the Word of God, but in time it is choked out by other things. . . . In this case, the stealing away of the potential fruit is a subtle and gradual process. . . .

Notice that Jesus didn't identify those choking weeds as "sins." He spoke of "the cares of this world and the deceitfulness of riches" that gradually strangle the once-healthy plant. *The Message* translates this as "weeds of worry and illusions about getting more and wanting everything under the sun."

The simple fact is that *good* things can occupy a person's time as well as bad things. And these worldly concerns may not be bad to begin with; they might be perfectly legitimate. They really only become "weeds" when they begin to crowd out and overshadow a man or woman's all-important relationship with God and get in the way of spiritual growth. (*Following Jesus in the Modern World*, 131–132)

12. What are some of "the cares of this world" that try to crowd out the time and attention you want to give to God?

13. What are some realistic things a person can do about this situation?

The fourth type of soil is "Fruitful Hearers."

But he who received seed on the good ground is he who hears the word and understands it, who indeed bears fruit and produces: some a hundredfold, some sixty, some thirty. (Matthew 13:23)

———————————————

This parable is found in three of the Gospels, and each one of the accounts gives us a little bit more understanding about this final category.

Here in Matthew, the good hearer is someone who *hears the word and understands it.* In Mark 4:20, he is described as one who *accepts* the Word. That means he takes it in, and it becomes a part of him. In Luke 8:15, the good hearer is said to be the one who *keeps* the Word. In other words, he holds on to it and practices it in his life. . . .

Again, in Matthew's version of this parable, the good hearer . . . hears it, follows it through from beginning to end, and thinks about it. It's like chewing your food rather than swallowing it whole. . . . The idea is that we are to think about the Word, ponder the Word, and meditate on the Word day and night. (*Following Jesus in the Modern World,* 136–137)

14. Chewing on the Word of God—both in a focused time each day and also throughout the day as we do other things—is an essential part of following Jesus. Quality pondering is often of more value than quantity reading (although reading whole books for the big picture is also a terrific thing to do).

There are lots of strategies for quality chewing and digesting. If you're using this study on your own, you could take the passage below and write out a prayer to God that builds on it, or put it into your own words, or choose one phrase and write what comes to mind when you think about it. You can set it to music or take it with you on a walk.

If you're meeting with a group, have the leader read the passage aloud. Then allow two full minutes of silence for people to think about one word or phrase from the passage that God is shining a spotlight on. Then let the leader read it again, and allow another two full minutes for people to talk with God silently about what that word or phrase is saying to them. Then let the leader read it again, and this time anyone who wants to pray aloud about the passage may do so. They can thank God for the word or phrase they've been thinking about, or they can say what they think God wants them to do about it, or they can ask God for something related to it.

Here's the passage:

Come to Me, all you who labor and are heavy laden, and I will give you rest. Take My yoke upon you and learn from Me, for I am gentle and lowly in heart, and you will find rest for your souls. For My yoke is easy and My burden is light. (Matthew 11:28-30)

4
GET OUT OF THE BOAT

To prepare for this discussion, please read chapters 8 through 10 of *Following Jesus in the Modern World*.

BY NOW, JESUS' disciples had been with Him for some time. They had heard Him teach and had seen what He could do. He had even sent them out on their own to tell people about the kingdom of God (see Matthew 10). They still had a long way to go, but Jesus didn't wait for people to become mature before they exercised their faith muscles. Exercising their muscles would help them become mature. In this session we'll look at two opportunities He gave His disciples to participate in His ministry.

Jesus took His disciples away to a remote place. John the Baptist had just been killed, and Jesus wanted time to pray. But the crowds followed Him to the remote place, hoping to see more miracles. Here's what happened then:

> And when Jesus went out He saw a great multitude; and He was moved with compassion for them, and healed their sick. When it was evening, His disciples came to Him, saying, "This is a deserted place, and the hour is already late. Send the multitudes away, that they may go into the villages and buy themselves food."

Notes and Observations

But Jesus said to them, "They do not need to go away. You give them something to eat."

And they said to Him, "We have here only five loaves and two fish."

He said, "Bring them here to Me." Then He commanded the multitudes to sit down on the grass. And He took the five loaves and the two fish, and looking up to heaven, He blessed and broke and gave the loaves to the disciples; and the disciples gave to the multitudes. So they all ate and were filled, and they took up twelve baskets full of the fragments that remained. Now those who had eaten were about five thousand men, besides women and children. (Matthew 14:14-21)

We read in verse 14 that Jesus "was moved with compassion for them." . . . These people were effectively thrill seekers. They were in it to be dazzled and entertained. But even though they were fickle and maybe had mixed motives, Jesus had compassion on them. The word translated *compassion* here means "to have your inner being stirred." . . .

And by the way, compassion is not just caring; it is caring enough to do something. It is not just pity. Compassion is pity *plus* action. Jesus had compassion on these multitudes, and He saw they were hungry. (*Following Jesus in the Modern World*, 161–162)

1. Do you know anyone who is strong in compassion? How does that person demonstrate compassion?

2. Why is it important to care for people's physical needs, not just their spiritual ones?

There always will be situations in life in which you and I will not have the resources or ability to respond. There will be times when we are in over our heads, out of our depth, and beyond our capacity. Such times as these will serve as tests in our lives. Have we really learned anything about walking with a faithful, powerful, loving God? Have we learned to trust Him? Have we learned to walk by faith when the way seems dark before us? . . .

Can you trust God? You must. God will allow us to enter into situations where the only way out is Him. And then, after He enables us to escape the inescapable and accomplish the impossible, He will get the glory. (*Following Jesus in the Modern World*, 175–176)

3. Think of a time when you didn't have the resources to deal with a situation. What was your first reaction? What did you ultimately do? What role (if any) did God play in what you did and what ultimately happened?

Do you ever find yourself (like me) having to relearn the same life lessons, again and again? Maybe when you were younger, the Lord taught you to trust Him for His provision, and you did. But now, as you've gotten older and have enjoyed a stable income for a number of years, maybe it's time to relearn that lesson.

Notes and Observations

Or maybe there was a time in your life when you didn't know the will of God, and you sought after Him with all your heart and waited on Him for direction. But some time has passed since those days, and you find that you're not relying on Him as you once did. Days slip by, and you realize that you haven't been opening the Word or seeking Him in prayer as you once did. And God has to reteach you — perhaps through some trying circumstances — what it means to be completely dependent on Him once again. (*Following Jesus in the Modern World*, 164)

4. How (if at all) is the challenge of depending on God different for you now than it was when you were younger?

Where was [the food in Matthew 14:20-21] coming from? How was this miracle accomplished? . . . I think the disciples would go out, distribute a basketful, come back, and there would be more. Then they would hand that out, and there would be more . . . and more and more and more, until everyone was satisfied.

God gives us what we need when we need it, not necessarily before — and never after — but when it is needed.

You might find yourself struggling with some anxious situations in your life right now. And you say, "What would I do if *this* happens?" "How would I ever handle it if *that* happens?" Or maybe, "What would I do if this situation came or this opportunity arose?"

The lesson is simply this: The Lord will give you what you need when the need is there. For right now, He will give you what need for the moment. Your responsibility is to simply bring your loaves and fishes to Jesus. (*Following Jesus in the Modern World*, 169–170)

5. What are some future possibilities that you tend to worry or speculate about? How do those thoughts affect you in the present?

6. How is the story of the loaves and fishes relevant to those concerns?

God gives to each one of us certain gifts and abilities, and the simple fact is that gifts don't come from God fully developed. You have to *use* them. You have to apply them. You have to practice and gain experience. Sometimes discovering your abilities and gifts is as simple as discovering what you're *not* good at.

It may be a humbling experience, but a lot of times we simply have to go out there, get our hands dirty in the work of the Lord, and find out what we're not particularly good at. You roll up your sleeves and try things. And after a while, with the help of the Holy Spirit and the counsel of others, you can determine how effective you are at what you do.

Then, after you've worked in several different capacities, you find out, "Hey, this is really working. I enjoy it. People are being blessed. God has made me good at this!" Then take that gift, develop it, and cultivate it. (*Following Jesus in the Modern World*, 170–171)

7. What are some of the attitudes that can keep a person from rolling up his or her sleeves and trying things in God's service?

Right after he tells us how Jesus fed five thousand people, Matthew tells us about Peter's spectacular failure:

Immediately Jesus made His disciples get into the boat and go before Him to the other side, while He sent the multitudes away. And when He had sent the multitudes away, He went up on the mountain by Himself to pray. Now when evening came, He was alone there. But the boat was now in the middle of the sea, tossed by the waves, for the wind was contrary.

Now in the fourth watch of the night Jesus went to them, walking on the sea. And when the disciples saw Him walking on the sea, they were troubled, saying, "It is a ghost!" And they cried out for fear.

But immediately Jesus spoke to them, saying, "Be of good cheer! It is I; do not be afraid."

And Peter answered Him and said, "Lord, if it is You, command me to come to You on the water."

So He said, "Come." And when Peter had come down out of the boat, he walked on the water to go to Jesus. But when he saw that the wind was boisterous, he was afraid; and beginning to sink he cried out, saying, "Lord, save me!"

And immediately Jesus stretched out His hand and caught him, and said to him, "O you of little faith, why did you doubt?" And when they got into the boat, the wind ceased.

Then those who were in the boat came and worshiped Him, saying, "Truly You are the Son of God." (Matthew 14:22-33)

8. What can we admire about what Peter does in this story?

At this point, the sea was still raging, and the wind was still screaming in the boat's rigging. Yet Peter was willing to literally step over the side of the boat into that wild storm because He was looking at Jesus. And that gave him confidence and courage.

Notice that Peter didn't take this action presumptuously. He didn't say, "Hang on, Lord, I'm coming! Here goes nothing!"

No, he asked Jesus for permission to come. I think Jesus had to smile. How could he not?

"Come on, Peter. Come on over here to Me."

Peter took several steps, and then . . . he sank. Yes, it was a failure, but what a failure! If you're going to fail, this is the way to do it. It was a spectacular, amazing failure, and we're still talking about it after two thousand years. (*Following Jesus in the Modern World*, 185)

9. Peter sank because he took his eyes off Jesus, saw the wind, and got scared (see verse 30). What are some of the things that can scare us so that we sink?

10. In practical terms, how does a person go about keeping his or her eyes on Jesus in one of these risky situations?

Do you think that this failure of Peter's came as a surprise to Jesus? Of course not. The Lord knew all about Peter. He had his number, and He had his number on the day He called him and gave him his new name: Peter, or Rock. But Jesus also knew what Peter would *become*. He didn't just see him for what he was; He saw him for what he would one day be.

That is how God sees you. You and I get obsessed sometimes with our shortcomings and flaws. When we walk in front of a mirror, most of us immediately notice all the things wrong with us. God looks at you and says, "I see what you will become. You just see a blank canvas, but I see a finished piece of art. A masterpiece! You just see a lump of coal, but I see a multifaceted diamond." (*Following Jesus in the Modern World*, 189)

11. What did Peter do when he realized he was failing? Was that a good idea? Why or why not?

12. What are some good ways to respond when we realize we are failing? How shouldn't we respond to failure?

Just as Peter was sinking, immediately Jesus stretched out His hand and caught him, and said to him, "O you of little faith, why did you doubt?" (Matthew 14:31).

In the original Greek, those two words translated "little faith" in our Bibles are one word: *littlefaith*. There is almost a tenderness to it—like a nickname. *"All right, Littlefaith, hold on to My hand. You were doing so well! Why did you doubt?"*

Jesus reached down, lifted him up, they got into the boat, and the wind ceased. It doesn't say that Jesus picked up Peter and carried him back. That means Peter walked . . . at Jesus' side, holding His hand.

Not a bad way to move through life!

Sometimes we miss that fact that, yes, Peter had a failure in faith and sank a little, but he also got back up on that water and walked on it with Jesus back to the boat. (*Following Jesus in the Modern World*, 190)

13. Both of the stories in this session involve the disciples in partnership with Jesus. He was ultimately the one with the power to take care of business, but that doesn't mean the disciples could just sit passively while He did the work. To feed the people, they had to show up with the five loaves and two fish, and then trust Jesus to keep filling the baskets as they did the work of passing out the food. Later, Peter had to get out of the boat and keep his eyes on Jesus, and then cry out to Him when his weakness made things go wrong.

How are you in partnership with Jesus right now? What is your job, and what do you need to ask from Him? If you're meeting with a group, give each person a chance to answer this question, possibly in subgroups of three or four people. Then call out together for Him to act. Don't be embarrassed to really cry out to Him, and if you're scared or failing, don't be too proud to admit it.

5

PERSISTENT FAITH

To prepare for this discussion, please read chapters 11 and 12 of *Following Jesus in the Modern World*.

WHEN PETER PANICKED out there on the waves, Jesus called him *littlefaith* (see Matthew 14:31). But Jesus was impressed by the faith of the bleeding woman who dared to reach for Him in her need (see 9:22). Along with love, faith is one of the most important things Jesus looks for in those who follow Him. If that's true, then what is faith? In this session we'll discuss two situations in which Jesus taught His followers what real faith looks like.

Notes and Observations

What is faith?

Sometimes we make it a little bit too mystical. In reality, faith is something we use every day and apply wherever we go.

When we go into a restaurant, we apply faith when we make that order. We have faith that the kitchen staff (totally invisible to our eyes) will prepare our food properly, use healthy ingredients, and follow normal hygiene standards. . . .

How much faith do we place in these things?

A very great deal of faith.

Notes and Observations

We actually place our very lives in their hands! (*Following Jesus in the Modern World*, 193)

1. Hebrews 11:1 says, "Faith is the confidence that what we hope for will actually happen; it gives us assurance about things we cannot see" (NLT). Give one or two examples of things you hope for that you're confident will actually happen.

2. How does that confident assurance about these things affect what you do?

Faith is a *confident assurance*. It's our title deed to everything God has done for us and provided for us. Sometimes we treat faith as though it were something fragile, like a museum piece or an egg. "Don't jostle my faith! Don't breathe on it! Don't touch it! You might break it!"

No, faith isn't like an egg. Faith is like a muscle that gets stronger through use. As any weightlifter knows, muscles actually build up when you break them down by using them. If you don't use your muscles, they will atrophy. In the same way, faith is something you need to *apply*—put to work—not something decorative you put on top of your bookshelf and dust off every few weeks.

Faith implies movement. It's something that you need to *use*. It is a living, restless thing, always moving toward its object. Faith can't remain inoperative or it will shrivel. We must *use* it. (*Following Jesus in the Modern World*, 194–195)

3. What are some activities or situations that force us to exercise our faith muscles?

Jesus traveled to an area outside Israel where He knew most of the people were non-Jews who worshipped false gods. Up to now, His ministry had been to His fellow Jews, but here He was, dragging His Jewish disciples into enemy territory. Why? This is what happened:

Then Jesus went out from there and departed to the region of Tyre and Sidon. And behold, a woman of Canaan came from that region and cried out to Him, saying, "Have mercy on me, O Lord, Son of David! My daughter is severely demon-possessed."

But He answered her not a word.

And His disciples came and urged Him, saying, "Send her away, for she cries out after us."

But He answered and said, "I was not sent except to the lost sheep of the house of Israel."

Then she came and worshiped Him, saying, "Lord, help me!"

But He answered and said, "It is not good to take the children's bread and throw it to the little dogs."

And she said, "Yes, Lord, yet even the little dogs eat the crumbs which fall from their masters' table."

Then Jesus answered and said to her, "O woman, great is your faith! Let it be to you as you desire." And her daughter was healed from that very hour. (Matthew 15:21-28)

4. Jesus was silent after this pagan woman cried out for His help. What effect did His silence have on His disciples?

5. What effect did it have on the woman?

Why was He delaying in giving her an answer? It may have been to provide an example for His own disciples. *"Littlefaith Peter, are you paying attention? Watch what this woman does! Watch how nothing discourages or deters her!"* (*Following Jesus in the Modern World*, 202)

6. It was shocking for a rabbi to talk with even a good Jewish woman in public, but Jesus was talking with a pagan woman. What do you imagine went on in His disciples' minds after He praised this woman's faith and gave her what she asked for?

If you have real faith, there will be *evidence* of that faith in your life. . . . Galatians 3:11 says, "The just shall live by faith." It doesn't say they will live by feelings, nor does it say they will live by circumstances. No, the just will live *by faith.* Faith can make the difference between something happening and not happening.

Yes, God is the one who does the work, but He chooses to accomplish that work primarily through human means.

For instance, the Lord could have sovereignly caused the Red Sea to part for the Israelites without the help of Moses. He didn't really need Moses to stretch out his staff over the water. Nevertheless, God chose to make Moses an integral part of it all. He told Moses, "Raise your staff and stretch out your hand over the sea to divide the water so that the Israelites can go through the sea on dry ground" (Exodus 14:16, NIV). (*Following Jesus in the Modern World*, 195–196)

7. How did the woman in Matthew 15 show evidence of great faith? Why do we call it faith and not groveling?

8. Do you think Jesus believed non-Jews were only dogs, and this woman got Him to change His mind? Why or why not?

If God doesn't seem to be answering a prayer of yours, here are five possible reasons why He's silent:

- A spiritual battle may be raging that you know nothing about.
- There may be unconfessed sin in your life that is hindering your prayer.
- There may be an idol in your life you need to deal with.
- God may want to draw you closer and keep you praying, as Jesus did with the woman in Matthew 15. He erected barriers that only genuine, persistent faith can hurdle, and He knew she would rise to the occasion.

- God may want someone else to learn something from the way you deal with the situation, as Jesus wanted His disciples to learn something from the Canaanite woman.

9. Given all these possible reasons for delays in answered prayer, what do you think we should do if we're praying for something and nothing seems to be happening?

10. An idol is any person, place, thing, or activity in your life that you have placed before your relationship with God. How can we tell if something has become an idol for us? What are some of the signs?

We've been looking at persistent faith. Now let's look at another important quality: childlike faith.

At that time the disciples came to Jesus, saying, "Who then is greatest in the kingdom of heaven?"

Then Jesus called a little child to Him, set him in the midst of them, and said, "Assuredly, I say to you, unless you are converted and become as little children, you will by no means enter the kingdom of heaven. Therefore whoever humbles himself as this little child is the greatest in the kingdom of heaven." (Matthew 18:1-4)

Small children can be incredibly self-centered, of course. But they are humble in this sense:

> A little child knows he or she needs help. They know they need you to pick them up when they get tired of walking on those little legs. They know that you will be the one who takes them out of the car seat and puts them back in the car seat. They know they need you to change their diaper, cut up their food, help them get into their clothes, or comfort them when they're scared in the middle of the night. They depend on you. They understand that, and they're fine with that.
>
> So Jesus was saying, "Just as a little child is happily dependent on his parent, so you should be dependent upon Me." Referring to their argument, He tells the disciples that the way to be strong is to recognize their innate weakness, and the way to greatness is along the path of humility. (*Following Jesus in the Modern World*, 215–216)

11. What do you think it means to humble ourselves the way a little child is humble? What attitudes and actions does this involve?

12. Why is this often hard for adults to do?

> Jesus said, "Whoever exalts himself will be humbled, and he who humbles himself will be exalted" (Matthew 23:12).
>
> That sounds like a really good plan to me.
>
> I would much rather get down on my knees before the Lord in real humility than, in my pride, have the Lord force me to my knees (or flat on my face). In other words,

Notes and Observations

don't wait for God to humiliate you, perhaps allowing circumstances in your life that will reveal to you and everyone else how weak you really are. (*Following Jesus in the Modern World*, 216)

13. How is humility related to faith? Is it possible to have proud faith? Explain.

14. Sometimes we read a story like the one about the Canaanite woman in Matthew 15, and we're put off by how completely she was willing to abandon her pride and beg for help from Jesus. We may not even like Jesus for making her do this. What do you think it is about us or our society that is so uncomfortable with that kind of lowliness before Jesus?

15. What do you need from God? How badly do you want it? If you're using this study on your own, consider getting on your knees to ask Him, if that's not already a posture you commonly take before Him. How easy is it for you to completely humble yourself before God?

If you're meeting with a group, how can you foster a genuinely humble atmosphere when you go to God in prayer together? (Kneeling is great, and expressions of emotion too, as long as you're not encouraging each other to show off.) Give it a try, and see what happens.

6

HOW NOT TO FOLLOW

To prepare for this discussion, please read chapters 13 and 14 of *Following Jesus in the Modern World*.

THERE'S A STORY about a wilderness guide who couldn't always remember the safe trail through the backcountry. When he got to a fork in the trail, he would leave you and your belongings there and go down one of the possible paths to check. Hours later he would return, often soaking wet up to his belly or with his jacket ripped to shreds. "Not that way! Not that way!" he would shout, and then you would know to follow him down the other path.

We can often learn as much from a bad example as from a good one. In this session we'll look at two bad examples. One is an example of how not to pray, and the other shows us how not to respond to an invitation from God.

1. If you found out you had six months to live, what is one thing you would do differently than you're doing now?

Notes and Observations

Notes and Observations

In Matthew 20, the mother of two of Jesus' disciples went to Him with a request for her sons. She loved her sons and was ambitious for them:

> *Now Jesus, going up to Jerusalem, took the twelve disciples aside on the road and said to them, "Behold, we are going up to Jerusalem, and the Son of Man will be betrayed to the chief priests and to the scribes; and they will condemn Him to death, and deliver Him to the Gentiles to mock and to scourge and to crucify. And the third day He will rise again."*
>
> *Then the mother of Zebedee's sons came to Him with her sons, kneeling down and asking something from Him.*
>
> *And He said to her, "What do you wish?"*
>
> *She said to Him, "Grant that these two sons of mine may sit, one on Your right hand and the other on the left, in Your kingdom."*
>
> *But Jesus answered and said, "You do not know what you ask. Are you able to drink the cup that I am about to drink, and be baptized with the baptism that I am baptized with?"*
>
> *They said to Him, "We are able."*
>
> *So He said to them, "You will indeed drink My cup, and be baptized with the baptism that I am baptized with; but to sit on My right hand and on My left is not Mine to give, but it is for those for whom it is prepared by My Father." (verses 17-23)*

2. What did this mother ask for? What do you think she meant by this request?

3. Not long before this, Jesus had said, "Therefore whoever humbles himself as this little child is the greatest in the kingdom of heaven" (Matthew 18:4). How well did these disciples and their mother understand that statement? How can you tell?

Why was this such a bad prayer?

Because it was utterly selfish. . . .

Jesus had just revealed that He would soon die by crucifixion, one of the most horrific, agonizing executions imaginable. Everybody knew what that meant. Crucifixion wasn't designed to merely end a life; it was a very slow death, designed to inflict the maximum amount of torture on a person. It was also designed to humiliate, as the crucified person would be hanging on a cross by the side of a Roman road for all to walk by, mock, and laugh at.

So this was a selfish prayer, to say the least, and offered at a very inopportune moment.

Jesus responded with a powerful question of His own in verse 22: "You don't know what you are asking! Are you able to drink from the bitter cup of suffering I am about to drink?" (NLT).

They replied, "We are able!"

You would think they might have paused for a moment before answering the Lord's question. Before saying, "Oh yes, we're able," they might well have asked, "Umm . . . what cup are You talking about here? Maybe You should define this cup before we say yes."

But they answered quickly, even though they had no idea what they were asking for. (*Following Jesus in the Modern World*, 236, 238)

4. Matthew 27:38 says that when Jesus was crucified, "Then two robbers were crucified with Him, one on the right and another on the left." What does this tell us about the cup Jesus was talking about in 20:22?

5. Not all prayers about things we want for ourselves are selfish. Give some examples of prayers we could pray for ourselves that are completely appropriate. Then give some examples of selfish prayers. How can we tell when a prayer is selfish?

We might find ourselves wondering, *What's the objective of praying? Am I really telling God anything He doesn't already know? Am I actually going to convince God to do something He doesn't necessarily want to do?*

The answer to those two last questions is no. God knows all things, and God will do what He wants to do.

So why should we even pray?

Prayer should be thought of as a relationship between a father and child. Prayer's value is that it keeps us in touch with God, keeps us walking and talking with Him through the days of our lives. . . . We need to be coming back each day for God's help, "so that we may receive mercy and find grace to help us in our time of need" (Hebrews 4:16, NIV). . . .

The principal objective of prayer is to get my will into alignment with God's will. Once that takes place, I will see my prayers answered more often in the affirmative. (*Following Jesus in the Modern World*, 232–234)

6. How can the act of praying help to get our will into alignment with God's will? If you've ever experienced that, describe how the process went.

Our second example of what not to do if we want to follow Jesus is a story He told about a generous king and those who rejected his kindness with flimsy excuses.

And Jesus answered and spoke to them again by parables and said: "The kingdom of heaven is like a certain king who arranged a marriage for his son, and sent out his servants to call those who were invited to the wedding; and they were not willing to come. Again, he sent out other servants, saying, 'Tell those who are invited, "See, I have prepared my dinner; my oxen and fatted cattle are killed, and all things are ready. Come to the wedding."' But they made light of it and went their ways, one to his own farm, another to his business. And the rest seized his servants, treated them spitefully, and killed them. But when the king heard about it, he was furious. And he sent out his armies, destroyed those murderers, and burned up their city. Then he said to his servants, 'The wedding is ready, but those who were invited were not worthy. Therefore go into the highways, and as many as you find, invite to the wedding.' So those servants went out into the highways and gathered together all whom they found, both bad and good. And the wedding hall was filled with guests." (Matthew 22:1-10)

7. What does it mean to "make light of" the king's invitation?

Notes and Observations

8. What point is Jesus making in this parable? Who is the king? Who are the invited guests who make light of the invitation?

> A reason is what we offer when we are unable to do something. An excuse is what we offer when we don't *want* to do something and hope to get out of it. (*Following Jesus in the Modern World*, 250)

9. Here are some excuses for not following Christ passionately and consistently. What is wrong with each excuse?

Excuse: Possessions are more important than God.

Excuse: Career is more important than God.

Excuse: A relationship is more important than God.

> And then we will offer up excuses as to why we can't read the Bible.
> "I'm just so busy these days. Life is so full. I just can't find the time."
> "The Bible is so big . . . I just don't know where to start."
> "I tried to read it, but there are some parts I don't understand."

"We read the Bible in church on Sunday. Doesn't that count?"

Those are excuses. Not reasons.

Let's imagine you got a call this week from your doctor, who said, "You need to make an appointment with me. I've reviewed those tests we did on you, and we need to talk."

Then further imagine that you learned you only had mere weeks to live. If you found yourself looking eternity in the face like that, do you think your schedule might flex a little, allowing you time to open the Bible? Of course it would! You would realize that the afterlife was almost upon you, and you would need God's perspective, God's comfort, and God's peace to face the days ahead.

It all depends on your perspective, because *we will make time for what is important to us. (Following Jesus in the Modern World,* 260–261)

10. Do you agree or disagree with this statement: "We will make time for what is important to us"? Why?

So what's the antidote for offering up weak, self-serving excuses? . . .

The word *disciple* comes from the root word *discipline,* which certainly includes the idea of making time for what is truly important. In contrast to the people in this story who offered up see-through excuses for not attending the king's banquet, true disciples prioritize God in their lives. They make time for God's Word, time for prayer, and time for being with God's people.

The answer to weak, deceptive excuses is to keep Jesus at the very center of our lives. *(Following Jesus in the Modern World,* 261–263)

Notes and Observations

11. How can we treat careers and relationships as important while still giving top priority to God? What are some of the things we'll do and not do?

12. Having looked at these two examples of what not to do — selfish, ill-considered prayers and deceptive excuses for ignoring God — what is one thing you want to do in response?

13. If you're meeting with a group, how can the group support you in prayer? (Don't hesitate to ask for prayer for yourself because you're afraid of being selfish. God will sort it out.)

7

HEAVEN AND EARTH

To prepare for this discussion, please read chapters 15 and 16 of *Following Jesus in the Modern World*.

THERE HAS RECENTLY been a lot of interest in books by people who, while unconscious and near death, have had experiences of heaven. The Bible tells us that heaven is real and Jesus rose from the dead to assure us that life after this life is real, but still a lot of readers feel reassured by the testimony of people who are on this earth now. Whether they have lost loved ones or are concerned about their own deaths, they are anxious to know, *will my loved ones and I be okay?*

In this session we'll look at something Jesus said about heaven. We'll also talk about something at least as important: how we live our lives here and now in light of our hope of heaven.

1. When you were a child, what did you believe about heaven? Or what impressions did you have about it, if any?

Notes and Observations

Notes and Observations

The same day the Sadducees, who say there is no resurrection, came to [Jesus] and asked Him, saying: "Teacher, Moses said that if a man dies, having no children, his brother shall marry his wife and raise up offspring for his brother. Now there were with us seven brothers. The first died after he had married, and having no offspring, left his wife to his brother. Likewise the second also, and the third, even to the seventh. Last of all the woman died also. Therefore, in the resurrection, whose wife of the seven will she be? For they all had her."

Jesus answered and said to them, "You are mistaken, not knowing the Scriptures nor the power of God. For in the resurrection they neither marry nor are given in marriage, but are like angels of God in heaven. But concerning the resurrection of the dead, have you not read what was spoken to you by God, saying, 'I am the God of Abraham, the God of Isaac, and the God of Jacob'? God is not the God of the dead, but of the living." (Matthew 22:23-32)

2. The word *resurrection* means to return to life in bodily form. Many non-Jews in Jesus' day believed they would one day be disembodied souls, but here Jesus specifically spoke of bodily resurrection. Why do you suppose many people feel more comfortable with the idea of an afterlife without a body?

When you are in heaven, it will be *you* who is in heaven. The real you. The complete you. You will have the same thoughts, feelings, and desires, but they will be perfected. After Christ rose again from the dead, He wasn't another Jesus. He was the same Jesus in His glorified state. In Luke 24, after He had been resurrected, Jesus said to His disciples: "Why are you troubled, and why do doubts rise in your minds? Look at my hands and my feet. It is I myself! Touch me and see" (verses 38-39, NIV).

He was the same, yet there were differences too. He could now appear in a room and disappear at will (which must have been a little hard to get used to). . . .

The newly minted resurrection body the Lord will give us won't be just an earthly body that has been resuscitated, but a likeness of the earthly body that has been glorified. God will recover from the dust a body with a definite relationship to your earthly body, but it will be completely transformed to suit your new environment. (*Following Jesus in the Modern World*, 275–277)

3. If you and others are raised from the dead with glorified bodies, what are some things that will be possible for you that wouldn't be possible if you were just disembodied souls?

Jesus said, "For in the resurrection [people] neither marry nor are given in marriage, but are like angels of God in heaven" (Matthew 22:30). So we will be *like* angels in that we won't have exclusive intimate relationships as we do now. But we won't *be* angels. Angels are a completely different type of being.

4. Certain movies and books glamorize the idea of being an angel. Why do you suppose some people want to be angels instead of humans?

Notes and Observations

Sometimes people ask, "Will we recognize one another in heaven?"

Of course we will! In heaven we will know *more* than we do on earth, not less. . . . Your mind will be working at full capacity, the dark shadows and stains of sin will have been finally removed, and you will have supernatural knowledge beyond anything you ever experienced on earth. So we will know one another — and much better than ever before. . . .

But what about our wife or husband? Will we still be married in heaven?

That was essentially the question posed by the Sadducees. First of all, our former earthly relationships won't be the focus of heaven; God is the focus of heaven. We will worship Him, walk with Him, serve Him, enjoy Him, and He will be sufficient to meet all our needs, forever.

Nevertheless, God created us as social beings from the very beginning, and I don't imagine that will change. We will still enjoy our loved ones and our old friends while we make new friends with the millions of people and angels who will inhabit heaven with us for eternity. . . .

So no, spouses won't be married to each other like they are now. But we will still be connected to each other and related to each other. In fact, our relationships will be even stronger than they were on earth. (*Following Jesus in the Modern World*, 278–282)

5. How do you respond to the idea that while we'll still enjoy our loved ones and friends in heaven, we won't have the kind of exclusive relationship with our husband or wife the way we do here? What thoughts, emotions, or questions does that raise?

In verse 32, Jesus said, "God is not the God of the dead, but of the living." That's another way of saying that the person who has put their faith in Jesus Christ never dies.

In fact, everyone you have ever known is immortal, whether they were a believer, an unbeliever, an agnostic, or an atheist. Every Christian, every Buddhist, every Hindu, every Muslim, every Republican, and every Democrat lives forever.

But not everyone will live forever in the same place.

The real question remains, *"Where* will I live forever?"
(*Following Jesus in the Modern World*, 273)

6. How should we respond to the knowledge that we will all live forever, but not everyone will live forever in the same place?

Now let's think about how we live on earth in light of our hope of heaven. Here's what Jesus says:

One [of the Pharisees], a lawyer, asked Him a question, testing Him, and saying, "Teacher, which is the great commandment in the law?"

Jesus said to him, "'You shall love the LORD your God with all your heart, with all your soul, and with all your mind.' This is the first and great commandment. And the

Notes and Observations

second is like it: 'You shall love your neighbor as yourself.' On these two commandments hang all the Law and the Prophets." (Matthew 22:35-40)

If you love the Lord, you will love the things He loves.

The flip side of that is if you love the Lord, you will hate the things He hates. That's because His nature is becoming your nature. Psalm 97:10 says, "You who love the LORD, hate evil!" God hates sin, and we should do the same. In Romans 12:9, the Bible tells us to "abhor what is evil."

Sometimes we allow ourselves to be fascinated with evil. We will see something on the Internet or on TV and say to ourselves, *Whoa, what's this? I want to check this out a little.* We tell ourselves we're just doing a little research or "keeping informed," but in reality we should have nothing to do with these dark or disturbing stories and images. Turn it off. Push it way. Abhor evil. Don't allow yourself to be drawn to or fascinated by something that you know God hates. *(Following Jesus in the Modern World, 297)*

7. In Hebrew culture, the heart is the core of your being, where your deepest motivations and will lie. If you love God with all your heart, what are some things you will naturally do?

8. What are some things you won't do if you love God with all your heart?

9. If you love God with all your mind, what are some things you will do?

Another thing to keep in mind is that if you love God, you will love other people in the family of God. Don't tell me you love God, whom you can't see, when you refuse to love people, whom you can see. Your love for God isn't real if you hate other Christians. The apostle John highlighted this fact in 1 John 3:14: "If we love our Christian brothers and sisters, it proves that we have passed from death to life. But a person who has no love is still dead" (NLT).

So don't talk about your love for God out of one side of your mouth while you are slandering or ripping apart another believer out of the other side of your mouth. If you love God, you'll love His kids. (*Following Jesus in the Modern World*, 298)

10. How will loving your neighbor as yourself affect what you do at work?

Notes and Observations

When you love someone, you naturally want to spend time with them. You enjoy their company and their companionship. When you hear of husbands and wives spending less time together or maybe taking separate vacations, that is not a good sign. (*Following Jesus in the Modern World*, 296)

11. What if you realize you don't long to spend time with God each day? What can you do about that?

In John 14:21, Jesus said, "He who has My commandments and keeps them, it is he who loves Me". . . . This isn't rocket science: If you love God, you will do what He says. (*Following Jesus in the Modern World*, 298)

12. What if you realize you haven't been loving God with your whole heart, soul, and mind, and so you haven't been doing what He says? What can you do about that? Give an example of what repentance looks like in practice.

13. When we want to turn to God in repentance, sometimes we have no idea what to say. It's helpful to have a vocabulary of repentance, not to mindlessly follow a script but as a place to begin. There are several great prayers of repentance in the Bible. Psalm 51 and Daniel 9:4-19 are two of them. There are also some historic prayers of repentance that build on the passages we have studied in this session. One of them is below. If you want to have a time of prayerful repentance on your own or with your group, you can use one of these prayers as a starting place.

Most merciful God,

we confess that we have sinned against You

in thought, word, and deed,

by what we have done,

and by what we have left undone.

We have not loved You with our whole heart;

we have not loved our neighbors as ourselves.

We are truly sorry and we humbly repent.

For the sake of Your Son Jesus Christ,

have mercy on us and forgive us;

that we may delight in Your will,

and walk in Your ways,

to the glory of Your Name. Amen.

Notes and Observations

8

THE CHOICE

To prepare for this discussion, please read chapters 17 through 19 of *Following Jesus in the Modern World*.

Notes and Observations

CHOICE IS SOMETHING we demand today. We love to have a big menu, and we love to have complete freedom to choose whatever we want. Some of us are quick to make up our minds, while others like to keep our options open for as long as possible.

This is fine when the choices are about lunch or our favorite toothpaste. When it comes to mint gel or tartar control, there is really no wrong choice. But in other cases there are good choices and bad choices, and trying to avoid the choice is a very bad idea. In this final session we're going to look at how three people decide—or try to avoid deciding—how to deal with who Jesus is.

None of these people has the luxury of making their decision in a vacuum. All three of them have others looking on, placing pressure on them. They have to reckon with what others will think of them. They will pay a stiff price if others disapprove. What will they do?

The first story is about Mary of Bethany, the sister of Martha and Lazarus. Jesus was at dinner with them, and everybody at the dinner knew that a few miles away in Jerusalem, the authorities wanted Him dead.

Notes and Observations

When Jesus was in Bethany at the house of Simon the leper, a woman came to Him having an alabaster flask of very costly fragrant oil, and she poured it on His head as He sat at the table. But when His disciples saw it, they were indignant, saying, "Why this waste? For this fragrant oil might have been sold for much and given to the poor."

But when Jesus was aware of it, He said to them, "Why do you trouble the woman? For she has done a good work for Me. For you have the poor with you always, but Me you do not have always. For in pouring this fragrant oil on My body, she did it for My burial. Assuredly, I say to you, wherever this gospel is preached in the whole world, what this woman has done will also be told as a memorial to her." (Matthew 26:6-13)

1. The unnamed woman in this story is Mary. What did she do?

2. What does her action tell you about who she believed Jesus was and what she believed was going to happen to Him? How did her action tell you that?

3. What price did Mary pay to do what she did?

Most of us are very concerned about what people think of us. One of the main reasons we don't speak more about our faith in Christ is because we don't want people to think we're a fanatic or (worst of all) laugh at us. Or maybe we hold back from speaking the truth to a friend because we don't want that friend to be upset or angry with us.

That's also why we sometimes don't do the right thing, the thing we know in our hearts we ought to do, because the right thing wouldn't be popular, and people might have a bad opinion of us.

In Proverbs 29:25 we read, "Fearing people is a dangerous trap, but trusting the LORD means safety" (NLT). (*Following Jesus in the Modern World*, 306)

4. Are you concerned about what unbelievers will think of you if you talk about your faith in Christ? If so, what is your main concern? How does that affect what you say and do? If not, how does that affect what you say and do?

Why did she do it? Because she wanted to give the most precious thing she had to Jesus. It was effectively her life's savings. Pouring it out like that was an act of complete abandon, devotion, and adoration.

What is the most precious thing in your life now? Maybe it's a person, a loved one. Maybe you drive it, and it's sitting in your garage right now. Maybe it's your home, your hobby, your health, or your career. Whatever it may be, have you presented it to Jesus yet? Have you given it to Him, with your hands wide open?

The value of a gift isn't determined by how much it costs, but by how much it cost *you*. That flask of nard cost Mary everything and was something of great sentimental and monetary value. (*Following Jesus in the Modern World*, 310–311)

5. Think of the most precious thing or person in your life right now. What goes through your mind when you think about giving that thing or person to Jesus with your hands wide open? What would doing that involve?

Now let's turn from Mary to Peter. A few days after Mary's extravagant act of devotion, he and the other disciples were with Jesus at another dinner. It would be the last dinner they shared before Jesus' death. Judas left to tell the authorities where they could arrest Him, and then Jesus said this:

> "All of you will be made to stumble because of Me this night, for it is written:
>
> 'I will strike the Shepherd,
> and the sheep of the flock will be scattered.'
>
> But after I have been raised, I will go before you to Galilee."
>   Peter answered and said to Him, "Even if all are made to stumble because of You, I will never be made to stumble."
>   Jesus said to him, "Assuredly, I say to you that this night, before the rooster crows, you will deny Me three times."
>   Peter said to Him, "Even if I have to die with You, I will not deny You!"
>   And so said all the disciples. (Matthew 26:31-35)

6. What did Jesus mean when He said the disciples "will be made to stumble"?

Be careful of saying [as Peter did in this passage], "Oh, I would never do that. I'm really strong in that area. I would never commit that sin in a million years."

Yet that may be the very area where you will fall.

Don't ever put confidence in yourself, in your own strength of character, in your own value system, in your own sense of dignity, in your own common sense.

That's what Peter did.

The Lord told Jeremiah, "The heart is hopelessly dark and deceitful, a puzzle that no one can figure out" (Jeremiah 17:9, MSG). . . .

So don't put confidence in yourself. Cling to the Lord and walk in His protection. The simple fact is, an unguarded strength is a double weakness. (*Following Jesus in the Modern World*, 325)

7. Name a strength that someone might have. How could that strength be a potential weakness for someone who is overconfident in that area?

A few hours later, Jesus asked Peter to pray for protection against temptation. But Peter fell asleep. He underestimated how badly he needed that protection.

[Jesus] went a little farther and fell on His face, and prayed, saying, "O My Father, if it is possible, let this cup pass from Me; nevertheless, not as I will, but as You will."

Then He came to the disciples and found them sleeping, and said to Peter, "What! Could you not watch with Me one hour? Watch and pray, lest you enter into temptation. The spirit indeed is willing, but the flesh is weak." (Matthew 26:39-41)

Notes and Observations

8. Here Jesus explained why we need to consistently pray for protection from temptation: "The spirit indeed is willing, but the flesh is weak." What does that mean?

Then the crisis came: Armed men arrived to arrest Jesus. Peter was prepared to die fighting for Jesus, but he was completely unprepared when Jesus calmly let Himself be arrested. Peter was now not only unprotected but also confused, because his Lord hadn't done what he expected. So Peter followed the armed men—at a safe distance, he thought.

Now Peter sat outside in the courtyard. And a servant girl came to him, saying, "You also were with Jesus of Galilee."

But he denied it before them all, saying, "I do not know what you are saying."

And when he had gone out to the gateway, another girl saw him and said to those who were there, "This fellow also was with Jesus of Nazareth."

But again he denied with an oath, "I do not know the Man!"

And a little later those who stood by came up and said to Peter, "Surely you also are one of them, for your speech betrays you."

Then he began to curse and swear, saying, "I do not know the Man!"

Immediately a rooster crowed. And Peter remembered the word of Jesus who had said to him, "Before the rooster crows, you will deny Me three times." So he went out and wept bitterly. (Matthew 26:69-75)

Peter was trying to go undercover, keeping tabs on events without really committing himself one way or another. He thought he could just blend into the woodwork. Have you ever tried to be an undercover Christian? . . .

At this point, Peter was worn down, defeated, weak, and vulnerable. Yes, he was following Jesus, but at a distance. And following at a distance, Peter had become cold and was attracted to the warmth of a fire in the high priest's courtyard — *the enemy's fire.* . . .

Here was Peter's problem: He was in the wrong place with the wrong people about to do the wrong thing. That's what happens when we fall into sin. We're in the wrong places, hanging out with the wrong crowd. Before we know it, we're swept along and begin doing the wrong thing. (*Following Jesus in the Modern World*, 332–333)

9. What do you think were the factors that led Peter to deny that he knew Jesus? What made him vulnerable?

10. Everyone is tempted to sin. Even Jesus was tempted. What can we do to make it less likely that we will give in when we are tempted?

Notes and Observations

11. Peter betrayed Jesus, and he wept bitterly about it. But that wasn't the end of his story. Jesus forgave and restored him (see Mark 16:7; John 21:1-19). Why is this important for us to remember? What are some of the things that can tempt us to forget this when we sin?

Peter *wanted* another chance, and Jesus gave it to him. But it's possible to shut the door on Jesus and never open it again. That's what the Roman governor, Pontius Pilate, did when the Jewish high council brought Jesus to him and demanded that Pilate execute Jesus.

> Now Jesus stood before the governor. And the governor asked Him, saying, "Are You the King of the Jews?"
>
> Jesus said to him, "It is as you say." And while He was being accused by the chief priests and elders, He answered nothing.
>
> Then Pilate said to Him, "Do You not hear how many things they testify against You?" But He answered him not one word, so that the governor marveled greatly. (Matthew 27:11-14)

12. What was it about Jesus that shocked and unnerved Pilate?

The last thing the Roman governor wanted at that moment was some kind of conflict with the Jews. He'd already had a number of run-ins with the people, and he certainly didn't need to have negative reports getting back to Caesar in Rome.

History tells us that Pilate was a brutal man. . . . Normally he was a guy who could dish out death penalties with ease. . . . But when Pilate was confronted with Jesus, he found himself strangely torn. For political reasons, he didn't want to offend the religious leaders who had hauled Jesus into his court. But on the other hand, he *knew* — way down in his heart of hearts — that Jesus was an innocent Man and didn't deserve to die. . . .

What was he going to do with Jesus Christ? He had to decide, even though he didn't want to decide. (*Following Jesus in the Modern World*, 341–343)

13. What price would Pilate have paid if he had refused to execute Jesus? What would it have cost him to entertain the possibility that Jesus really was the King of Jews foretold by Jewish prophecy?

God gave Pilate every opportunity to take Jesus very seriously. Pilate's wife sent him a message that she'd had a dream about Jesus (see Matthew 27:19). Jesus told Pilate several things that should have gotten his attention (see John 18:28–19:12). But Pilate chose not to risk offending the powerful people who wanted Jesus dead.

When Pilate saw that he could not prevail at all, but rather that a tumult was rising, he took water and washed his hands before the multitude, saying, "I am innocent of the blood of this just Person. You see to it."

And all the people answered and said, "His blood be on us and on our children." (Matthew 27:24-25)

This is typical of so many people today. They want to put off what they don't want to deal with. But you cannot put off Jesus Christ. . . .

Notes and Observations

History tells us that seven years after this cruel, self-serving decision, Pilate was banished to Gaul by the emperor Caligula. Gaul was a distant region to the northwest of Italy, beyond the Alps. In that place, the historical records say, he suffered what appears to be a mental breakdown. And one night Pilate went out into the darkness and hung himself, just as Judas Iscariot had done.

What a tragic waste of life. He threw his life away because he was more concerned about what others thought about him than what God thought about him. His craving for popularity and power ended up costing him everything. (*Following Jesus in the Modern World*, 354–355)

14. What are some bad choices a person might make today because they're afraid to offend people at work or in another relationship?

15. Mary of Bethany chose to pay a price to worship Jesus. Peter chose to avoid paying the price—but later he changed his mind. Pilate also tried to avoid paying the price—and as far as we know, he never changed his mind.

If you're doing this study on your own, ask God if there are any hard choices He wants you to make. Go back over the things you've learned from this whole study, and see what stands out to you. You might want to write down those key insights and thank God for them. Then ask Him how He wants you to respond. Are there some priorities you need to adjust, some things you need to do more of or less of? Will that cost you something? What will it cost you *not* to do what God is prompting you to do?

If you're meeting with a group, encourage group members to think through these things on their own. If you've built up enough trust, you can talk about some of these hard choices. You can pray together for wisdom and courage to be like Mary—or if you've been Peter, to change course and straighten things out. Then thank God for the things you've learned from this study.

Notes and Observations

LEADER'S NOTES

IF THIS IS your first time leading a small-group discussion, don't worry. You don't need to know the perfect answers to the questions, and you don't need to be a Bible expert. What you do need is a willingness to read the corresponding portions of *Following Jesus in the Modern World* each week, look up the Bible passages you'll be studying, think about the questions ahead of time, and read these leader's notes. You also need to ask the Holy Spirit to work in your life and the lives of your group members.

LEADER'S JOB DESCRIPTION
Your role is to:

- *Help people bond as a group*, especially if they don't know each other well. The first question in each session usually invites people to say a little about themselves as they start thinking about the topic at hand. (In one case, there's a quiz for them to do on their own.) If people are shy, you can go first in answering question 1. Give a genuine answer, and keep it under one minute long. Ask everyone else to keep their answers to a minute rather than telling long stories so that this question doesn't consume all of your time. The intent here is to break the ice and get to know things about each other that don't usually come out in small talk. (Normally, you should *not* go first in answering the questions. Question 1 is the exception. If you routinely answer the questions, people will stay silent and act like your audience.)

- *Keep the discussion moving.* Encourage people to have a conversation rather than just going around the circle and sharing answers to each question. You can ask follow-up questions such as, "Why do you think that's the case?" "Can you say more about that?" "What do others think?" "Is there a particular place in Acts that supports that idea?" and "Does the book shed any light on this?"

- *Keep the group on track* when it's tempted to go off on a tangent. If people get bogged down on a question or go off topic, you can say, "I'm going to interrupt here and bring us back to the text." "Does anyone else have thoughts on question 2?" or "Let's go on to the next question. Could someone read it aloud?"

- *Make sure everyone gets a chance to talk* and that no one dominates. It's not necessary that every person respond aloud to every question, but every person should have the chance to do so. Sometimes it's necessary to interrupt a talkative person and say, "Thanks, Joe. What do others think?" You, too, should not dominate the discussion.

- *Make sure the discussion remains respectful.* See the ground rules under the upcoming "Guiding the Discussion" section.

- *Pray for your group.* Ask for the Holy Spirit to fill each person, increase their faith and courage, and empower them to share the gospel with those around them. Many of them may never have led someone to Christ. Ask God to do more through them than they can imagine.

PREPARING FOR THE DISCUSSION

Read the chapters from *Following Jesus in the Modern World* before each group meeting. If you can, work through your own responses to the discussion questions ahead of time. Even though you won't be sharing your answers each time, thinking through the questions will help you think of follow-up questions.

GUIDING THE DISCUSSION

A few ground rules can make people comfortable discussing what they really think:

- *Confidentiality:* Whatever is said in the group stays in the group. Nothing is to be repeated to those who weren't there.
- *Honesty:* We're not here to impress each other. We're here to grow and to know each other.
- *Respect:* Disagreement is welcome; disrespect is not.

Ask for a volunteer to read each question aloud before you discuss it. In some cases, it will be helpful to have someone read aloud the text between the questions.

Encourage people to talk to each other rather than to only you. When someone shares an answer, avoid replying with your own views. Instead, ask what others think. If someone says something seriously unbiblical, give others in the group a chance to say what is true rather than doing it yourself. If no one does, say something such as, "There's a Bible passage that sheds light on what we're discussing," and then tell them the Scripture to look for and ask a group member to read it aloud. Do your best to let the group arrive at what the Bible teaches, and take the role of teacher yourself only as a last resort.

Likewise, avoid the temptation to answer a question if others are silent. Don't be afraid of silence. Wait for the group. People often need time to think. If you answer the questions,

Notes and Observations

people will learn to wait for you, and discussion will be squelched. Sometimes it's helpful to rephrase the question in your own words. Then wait for others' responses.

There isn't enough space in this guide to give you suggested answers for all of the discussion questions, and in many cases group members will be talking about their own lives, so there isn't a single right answer. Therefore, in the notes below we've chosen some questions from each session to address. In some cases these notes will be guidance on how to handle a question, and in other cases they will suggest answers to questions that might be especially difficult. These answers aren't meant to be exhaustive, nor are they (in most cases) the only right answer. They're meant to help you if the group gets stuck or off track.

SESSION 1

Question 1. This question is an icebreaker to get the group thinking about what following means. You might want to go first to set an example of how long an answer is appropriate. If you stay well under one minute, but still say something substantive, then it's more likely that others will open up but won't tell long and irrelevant stories. In general, the leader shouldn't answer the questions, and definitely shouldn't go first, but with icebreaker questions at the beginning of the session it's sometimes helpful for the leader to answer.

Questions 2–3. Following involves action: doing the will of the Father. Hearing Jesus' teaching isn't enough. Mentally believing what the Bible says about Jesus isn't enough. Following is doing what Jesus said. This raises the question, "What did Jesus say we should do?" Apparently prophesying and doing wonders aren't the top of the list. Matthew 7:21-25 comes at the end of Matthew 5–7, in which Jesus spelled out what He wanted done: things like forgiving others, not feeding our lust, loving enemies, giving to the needy, praying without trying to impress others, and so on.

Question 4. See if you can come up with a list of practical ways to do what Jesus said in Matthew 5–7 in these various contexts.

Question 7. Some possibilities are fear of rejection, other people's preconceptions about Christianity, and busyness.

Question 10. We can panic. We can get angry or bitter at God, other people, and ourselves. We can get depressed. We can stop going to church and isolate ourselves. On the other hand, we can cry out to God for help. We can find a few people who will stand with us and pray with us while we work through sadness and confusion. We can seek out practical help and take steps to pursue medical treatment or a new job.

Question 11. Jesus promises to be with us always. He doesn't promise to make sure we always feel His presence. Sometimes He withdraws those good feelings so we can strengthen our faith muscles and not rely so much on feelings. Therefore, the lack of feeling His presence is not necessarily a sign that we are doing anything wrong. However, sometimes it's a result of sin, depression, or lack of time spent alone in prayer.

SESSION 2

Question 2. They were well aware that this title didn't mean Jesus was a son of God in the way that we are all God's children. They knew it meant that Jesus is God just as the Father is God, that Jesus has always existed, that the universe was created through Him, that He is God in human flesh.

Question 3. "The time" meant the time of judgment. Even though the book of Revelation hadn't been written, they already knew that Satan and all of his demons were going to face a final judgment and be thrown into the lake of fire (see Revelation 20:7-10).

Question 4. Submitting our lives to this truth involves first a posture of the heart: genuine, deep-down surrender to God. Then it involves actions consistent with that surrender: obedience to what Jesus says. You might want to explore what surrender and obedience mean in practice.

Notes and Observations

Question 8. It's important to create an atmosphere of honesty and trust in your group so that people who are not having happy feelings can say so. Some in your group will be feeling joy, but others won't, and being honest about that can help them grow in faith. Romans 12:15 tells us to rejoice with those who rejoice and mourn with those who mourn. A small group is the ideal place to do that. The lack of happy feelings about heaven is not the same as unbelief.

Question 9. Jesus is not angry or frustrated at people who are discouraged. In fact, when discouraged people are willing to take their discouragement to Him, He's thrilled. Your group should be a place where discouraged people can feel welcome to go to Jesus with you.

Question 10. John's disciples could tell him that they had seen Jesus fulfill verses 5-6, and verse 4 is an encouragement to John: be strong; don't be afraid; God is coming for you. John could deal with the likelihood of his own imminent death as long as he was sure the Messiah had truly come.

Question 11. We should trust Him because He has a track record of trustworthiness. He said He would rise from the dead, and He did. He said He would build His church, and He did. He said He would give courage to those in difficult situations, and He has done it over and over, even for people facing death.

SESSION 3

Question 2. This is a chance for group members to look at their hearts and dig into their schedules. On the heart side, spending time with Jesus is possible when we genuinely decide to make Him more of a priority than entertainment and accumulating possessions. On the practical side, we can start by noticing the time we give to surfing the Internet, nonessential texting, television, worry, brooding about things that annoy us, and so on. Ask group members to take a week and just notice that time. Even better: ask them to keep a log of time spent on

those things. They should write down how much time and
when. That information can then tell them when they have
pockets of time to devote to Jesus. For instance, instead of coming home from work and decompressing by surfing the Internet
for half an hour, we can come home from work and decompress
by going into a room, shutting the door, and writing Jesus an
e-mail about our day and saving it in a folder. Initially we may
not feel like doing that. But if Jesus is truly a priority, we are
capable of choosing this shift. Try doing some creative thinking
together about how to make time for Jesus.

Question 3. This question allows the group to acknowledge
that some people truly face heavier non-optional demands than
others. Mothers of babies and toddlers, for example, have
all-day, all-night responsibilities. Some people work twelve-hour
days just to provide their families with the basics. But it's worth
asking ourselves if our long hours are aimed at the basics or if
we are working so hard because we have an insatiable craving
for more and newer stuff.

Question 6. Again, this is a chance for creative brainstorm-
ing. Some people put hourly reminders into their phones so they
can have a two-minute check-in with Jesus every hour. They ask
themselves and God, "What role does God want in what I am
doing right now?" Other people check in with God first thing
in the morning, at noon, right after work, and before bed.
Developing a routine can be helpful in a busy life.

Question 8. Many people find it burdensome to love their
neighbors because that doesn't come naturally. They find it
burdensome to share their faith because it's scary. But those
burdens are nothing compared to the burden of getting yourself
stuck in an addictive behavior, or a destructive relationship, or
the treadmill of trying to accumulate enough material things
when nothing ever feels like enough.

Question 10. Some people go to church or Bible study to
spend time with people, or because they like the music, or
because they get an emotional high. These aren't bad things, but
they are without value if we're not seeking to do what Jesus says.

SESSION 4

Question 3. To save time, you might encourage people not to tell the whole story of the situation but to focus on how they reacted. For example, "A friend of mine lost his job, and he was spiraling into depression. My first reaction was to pray for him every day and also to give him lots of advice. But he didn't appreciate my advice, and I got tired of praying for the same thing every day and not seeing any change. I started distancing myself from him. Instead of talking with him after church as before, I talked to other people, and when we did talk, I didn't ask about the job search. Eventually I realized that because I had so little control over the outcome, I had stopped acting with compassion at all. So I started praying for my friend consistently again. And I made a point of spending time with him, involving him in things our family was doing, asking how he was doing, saying supportive things, and not trying to tell him what to do. I couldn't give him a job, but I could give him respect, so I focused on that. I needed a lot of help from God to keep praying and acting that way for months."

Question 4. If many in your group are still young in the faith, you could revise this to, "What is the main challenge you face in depending on God?" If people have trouble putting their thoughts into words, you could suggest some possibilities: "For instance, is it busyness? Are you afraid God won't come through for you? Do you feel that God has let you down in the past? Do you like to be in charge? Do you get impatient?"

Question 7. One person might be afraid of failure and embarrassment. Another might be preoccupied with his own wants and needs. Another might be uncomfortable in unfamiliar situations or with unfamiliar people.

Question 9. Lots of circumstances are scary: having to apply for a new job, trying a new area of ministry, getting married, getting an illness. These things can take our focus off Jesus and onto the bad things that might happen.

Question 10. There are lots of practical things we can do. One of the most basic is simply planning regular time alone with

God. And not just going through the motions, but really telling God how the risky situation is affecting us and what we need from Him. Praying the psalms can be helpful, because the psalmists both cry out to God and express reasons for trusting God.

Question 12. Failure is a learning experience. It's feedback. Anger, depression, and giving up are all unhelpful responses. Crying out to God and adjusting our course based on what we've learned from the feedback are good responses.

SESSION 5

Question 2. It's important to get the connection between faith and what we do. If you're confident that your bank's online bill-paying service will safely and properly deliver the money to your phone company, then you'll express that confidence by paying your bills that way. If you pay your bills through the mail, you're expressing confidence that the postal service will deliver the payment on time.

Question 3. Anything that is beyond our own resources forces us to exercise our faith muscles. A long illness. Something we want that we have to wait for. Going outside our comfort zone to help someone in need. Sharing our faith.

Questions 4–5. His silence made His disciples assume that He had no more respect or compassion for the woman than they did, so they said, "Send her away." However, it didn't make the woman believe He lacked compassion and respect. It made her cry out to Him even more, stretching her faith in His goodness.

Question 6. His disciples' heads were surely spinning. They had to decide whether their contempt for pagans and women was right and Jesus was wrong, or Jesus was right and their contempt was wrong. They had to come to grips with the fact that Jesus values faith in anybody, no matter how the rest of society views that person.

Question 8. If Jesus thought non-Jews were dogs, it's hard to explain why He traveled to minister in the non-Jewish region of Tyre and Sidon at all. Laurie writes,

Notes and Observations

I'm pretty sure this woman knew what was up and that Jesus eventually would give her what she needed. I think she could see the love in His eyes rather than hatred or rejection. I think she could hear the compassion in His voice. Perhaps she even detected a little smile. . . .

This Gentile woman pressed on and would not be discouraged. When the door was shut in her face, she just knocked at it. When Christ compared her to a dog, she accepted the comparison and asked Him to spare her a few crumbs from His table. She loved her child, and she would not take no for an answer. (*Following Jesus in the Modern World*, 207–208)

Question 9. We should keep praying and not lose heart. We should pray to have our will in alignment with God's, to know what He wants us to do and to have. We should examine our lives to see if sin or idolatry is hindering our prayer, but often delays have nothing to do with anything we're doing wrong.

Question 11. It means to actively depend on God the way a child has to depend on adults. The culture of Jesus' day was not child-centered. Children were viewed as very low in importance, and they were expected to defer to adults the way slaves deferred to masters. Jesus is telling His disciples to approach God not with demands but with the attitude that they have no right to demand anything. Instead of having faith that God will make our lives work out because He owes that to us, He wants us to see ourselves as totally dependent on Him, and have faith in Him because we need Him the way a child needs parents.

SESSION 6

Question 2. To sit at Jesus' right and left meant to have the number two and number three positions in the hierarchy.

Question 5. To ask for enough money for our basic needs and those of our family is appropriate. To ask to be rich or famous or powerful is rarely appropriate, because those aren't things God values. To ask for a project to be successful is appropriate if the project contributes something of value to the world. To ask to win at someone else's expense is definitely selfish.

Question 6. Sometimes saying aloud what we really want shows us whether it is a need, an innocent desire, or something that will just feed our ego. Praying over time can gradually peel away the righteous-seeming veneer of our desires and show us what our hearts truly want. It can take us from demanding to humble asking.

Question 8. When Jesus told the story originally, the king was God and the invited guests were the Jewish leaders who opposed Jesus. Today the story applies equally to Christians, and even to all people, because God's invitation has gone out to all.

Question 9. Take some time to unpack why possessions (or career, or relationships) aren't more important than God. What do we look to possessions to give us? Can they deliver? What does God offer that possessions can't? Why is God greater than material stuff, even if stuff makes us feel good and God doesn't?

Question 11. For instance, we'll work hard at our jobs, but if career advancement demands that we sacrifice time worshipping and learning from God, we'll choose God. If career demands that we make ethical compromises, we'll choose to do what is right over what gets us ahead.

SESSION 7

Question 1. This is an icebreaker question, so everyone should have a chance to respond briefly, but don't spend a lot of time commenting on each other's childhood impressions. The point of this question is to get the group thinking about the topic at hand and then to move on to the discussion of the Bible passage.

Question 2. There are many possible responses. Ideas and images from popular culture can be hard to shake off. Ideas from other religions, such as Hinduism and Buddhism, are also influential in our society, and those religions view the human body as a temporary burden that one leaves behind when one attains enlightenment. In addition, many people have a love-hate relationship with their bodies—which they see as ugly, or prone to pain and illness, or tempted to sins of the flesh, or limited in other ways.

Question 3. The point of imagining the possibilities here is to help people grasp that Jesus teaches a very embodied faith. The Bible is full of imagery about feasting at the Resurrection (see Isaiah 25:6-9). Bodily expressions of worship, music, creativity, physical affection between friends—all these things and more will be possible with glorified bodies.

Question 4. Again, there are many possible responses. It's fun to imagine transcending the limitations of our ordinary human lives. This can be innocent fun, or it can spring from the desire to be powerful enough to be independent of God, which was Eve's problem (see Genesis 3:5-6) and Lucifer's (see Isaiah 14:12-14).

Questions 7–9. We will enjoy worship and spending time alone with God. We will reject the allure of false gods like money and fame. We will act with justice and mercy in our personal lives and pursue them in society. We will be eager for God to uproot our character flaws. Loving God with our minds includes filling them with true and beautiful ideas and images, and avoiding images that debase us (think TV and Internet).

Question 11. Being honest with ourselves and God is half the battle. We should discipline ourselves to spend time with God daily regardless of our feelings, because our feelings shouldn't control us. But we should also notice those bored feelings and pray about them. We can ask God to enable us to desire Him more. We can also ask God to show us what is hindering us from enjoying Him.

Question 12. Revelation 2:5 tells us to *repent*, which means:

To change your direction, to go back to where you were before. Pull a U-turn in the middle of your life's highway and head back to where you got off course. You won't need your GPS unit to find the way, because God Himself will guide you to that place. (*Following Jesus in the Modern World*, 301)

SESSION 8

Question 2. It was customary at that time to wrap a dead body in linen glued together with fragrantly spiced ointment. Mary had a jar of spiced ointment that could be used for a wedding, funeral, or other special occasion. She poured it on Jesus to show love and worship—because she knew He was the Messiah who had raised her brother from the dead—and also to show she believed He was going to die. She apparently knew Jesus had been predicting His death to His disciples, and while they didn't quite believe Him, she apparently did.

Question 3. She paid the financial cost of this incredibly expensive ointment as well as the cost of humiliating herself in front of a roomful of friends and family. For an unmarried woman to publicly display affection for a man in any physical way was extremely shameful in her culture.

Question 5. This could involve selling something and giving the money to God. Or it could involve telling the Lord (and meaning it) that it really is okay with you to take this person or part of your life in whatever direction He wants. It could involve a change of direction or priority in your career or your use of time.

Question 6. He meant they would desert Him in the moment of crisis when He was arrested.

Question 7. For instance, a person who has always had enough money might be confident that he would never steal, and so might be placed in a position of trust with money. But if he suddenly finds himself in a financial crisis with the need for

Notes and Observations

immediate funds, he might be deeply and unexpectedly tempted to abuse that position of trust.

Question 8. In part, He meant the body is weak—the disciples were physically tired, and when we're tired or hungry, we truly are more vulnerable to making bad decisions or skipping good ones. But even more, He meant our human nature is weak—we naturally fear for our physical and emotional safety, we want to be loved and respected, and the tempter can play on our desires and fears to manipulate us.

Questions 9–10. See *Following Jesus in the Modern World* 325–336. Peter was overconfident, he skipped prayer, he trusted his own efforts instead of relying on God, he allowed distance between himself and God, and he was hanging out with the wrong people. We can strengthen ourselves by cultivating humility, dealing with our stress level so we don't get overtired, praying consistently, and so on.

Question 12. Jesus' silence when accused really got to Pilate. Most people either admit their guilt or argue their innocence. They aren't indifferent to attack and punishment.

Question 13. Pilate could have lost his job or even his life if the Jewish leaders had complained to Rome about him. Even more, everything he believed was true about the world would have been threatened if he had entertained the possibility that Jesus was the King of the Jews. It's very hard for someone to give up their long-held assumptions about reality.

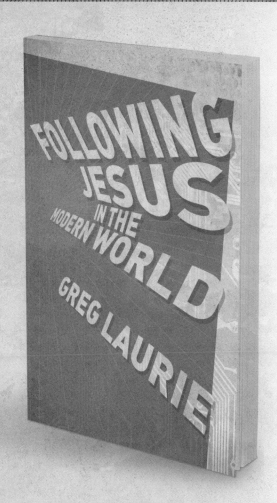

Other Books by Greg Laurie

As I See It
Better Than Happiness
Daily Hope for Hurting Hearts
Dealing with Giants
Deepening Your Faith
Discipleship—Start! To Follow
Essentials
Essentials 2
Essentials Bible Study
Following Jesus in the Modern World
For Every Season, volumes 1, 2, and 3
God's Design for Christian Dating
The Great Compromise
The Greatest Stories Ever Told, volumes 1, 2, and 3
Hope
Hope for America
Hope for Hurting Hearts
How to Know God
Living Out Your Faith
Making God Known
Married. Happily.
Red, the Color of Christmas
Run to Win
Secrets to Spiritual Success
Signs of the Times
Strengthening Your Faith
Ten Things You Should Know About God and Life
Upside Down Living
Upside Down Living Bible Study
What Every Christian Needs to Know
Why, God?
Worldview

Visit: www.AllenDavidBooks.com

KERYGMA
PUBLISHING